Nick Toczek lives in Bradford, where he breeds lizards and is a professional magician, puppeteer and storyteller. His first pantomime, *Sleeping Beauty's Dream*, has just been published, as has his second short novel for adults, *Group of Heroes*. Macmillan recently published *Kick It!*, a collection of his football poems.

Andrew Fusek Peters is 'an experienced and accomplished anthologist' *TES*. 'His anthologies are always exciting and interesting' *Books For Keeps*. With his wife Polly he has written and edited over thirty-five critically acclaimed books – poetry collections, plays, picture books, graphic novels and a verse novel. For more info on the tallest poet in the UK, check out www.tallpoet.com.

Axel Scheffler has achieved worldwide acclaim for his children's book illustration, and his books have been translated into over twenty languages. His most recent successes include *The Gruffalo*, *Room on the Broom*, *The Snail on the Whale* and *The Smartest Giant in Town*. Born in Germany, Axel now lives in London.

Other books from Macmillan

JOIN IN OR ELSE!
poems chosen by Nick Toczek

KICK IT!
football poems by Nick Toczek

HOW TO EMBARRASS GROWN-UPS
poems chosen by Paul Cookson

SPECTACULAR SCHOOLS
poems chosen by Paul Cookson and David Harmer

DINOS, DODOS AND OTHER DEAD THINGS
poems chosen by Brian Moses

THE DOG ATE MY BUSPASS

POEMS CHOSEN BY
NICK TOCZEK AND ANDREW FUSEK PETERS

ILLUSTRATED BY AXEL SCHEFFLER

MACMILLAN CHILDREN'S BOOKS

First published 2004 by Macmillan Children's Books
a division of Macmillan Publishers Limited
20 New Wharf Road, London N1 9RR
Basingstoke and Oxford
www.panmacmillan.com

Associated companies throughout the world

ISBN 0 330 41800 9

This collection copyright © Nick Toczek and Andrew Fusek Peters 2004
All poems copyright © the individual poets
Illustrations copyright © Axel Scheffler 2004

The right of Nick Toczek, Andrew Fusek Peters and Axel Scheffler to be identified as the compilers and illustrator of this work has been asserted by them in accordance with the Copyright, Designs and Patents Act 1988.

All rights reserved. No part of this publication may be reproduced, stored in or introduced into a retrieval system, or transmitted, in any form, or by any means (electronic, mechanical, photocopying, recording or otherwise) without the prior written permission of the publisher. Any person who does any unauthorized act in relation to this publication may be liable to criminal prosecution and civil claims for damages.

1 3 5 7 9 8 6 4 2

A CIP catalogue record for this book is available from the British Library.

Printed and bound in Great Britain by Mackays of Chatham plc, Kent

This book is sold subject to the condition that it shall not,
by way of trade or otherwise, be lent, re-sold, hired out,
or otherwise circulated without the publisher's prior consent
in any form of binding or cover other than that in which
it is published and without a similar condition including this
condition being imposed on the subsequent purchaser.

'Here Lies . . .' by Eric Finney, first published in *Dead Funny*, Collins; 'Reasons We Can't Get a Dog' by Steven Herrick from *Poetry to the Rescue*, University of Queensland Press, 1998; 'Excuse My Excuse' by Brian Patten reproduced by permission of the author c/o Rogers, Coleridge & White Ltd.; 'This Poem Apologizes' by Helen Dunmore reproduced by permission of A. P. Watt Ltd.

CONTENTS

Misleading Reading *Graham Denton*	1
The Astronaut's Apology *Penny Dolan*	2
The Vampire's Apology *John Foster*	3
The Last Boy to School *Dave Ward*	4
This is Why *Linda Lee Welch*	5
The Cloud's Lament *Celia Warren*	6
Open House *Hazel Townson*	7
The Computer's Excuse for Crashing *Andy Seed*	8
An Alien Ate My Homework *Kaye Umansky*	10
Barbara in the Shed *Jan Dean*	13
Nothing to Do with Me *Jane Saddler*	14
The Not-Me Kid *Nick Toczek*	16
Absence *Jill Townsend*	18
I'm Sorry that My Poem's Late *Ted Scheu*	19
This Poem Says Sorry *Stephen Clarke*	22

That's No Excuse! *Eric Finney*	23
Here Lies . . . *Eric Finney*	24
The Conjuror's Ghost *John Foster*	25
The Cow's Excuse *Roger Stevens*	26
The Worst Excuses in the World *Clare Bevan*	28
Excuse my Excuse *Brian Patten*	30
Who, Me? *Simon Pitt*	31
A Way with Words *Wes Magee*	32
It's a Goal! *John Hunter*	34
Reasons We Can't Get a Dog *Steven Herrick*	35
Out of the Blue *Damian Harvey*	36
Soldier, Soldier, Will You Marry Me? *Traditional*	38
Goldfish *Rachel Rooney*	40
No Time *Alison Chisholm*	41
Who Was Supposed to Feed the Hamster? *Jennifer Curry*	42
Oh, Am I Still Here? *Jan Dean*	44
This Poem Apologizes *Helen Dunmore*	46

An Easy Mistake *Patricia Leighton*	48
Broken Promise *Lucinda Jacob*	49
The Spider's Excuse *Steve Turner*	50
The Elastic's Apology *John Foster*	51
Why Are You Late for School? *Steve Turner*	52
Excuses, Excuses *Catharine Boddy*	53
I Don't Be-Leaf You *Polly Peters*	54
Black-eyed Susan *Andrew Fusek Peters*	55
The Slippery Truth *Andrew Fusek Peters*	56
A Note from Mum *Ann Bonner*	58
A Sorry Story *Clare Bevan*	60
Waiting for the Eyes to Return *Ian Souter*	62
The Wolf's Excuse *Yvonne Coppard*	64
A Diner Apologizes *Stewart Henderson*	66
A Washing Machine Apologizes *Clare Bevan*	68
Walkies *Mike Johnson*	72
First Things First *Clive Webster*	70
Too Risky *Clive Webster*	74

Writer's Excuse *Traditional*   75

One, Two, Three, Four, Five *Traditional*   76

The Most Complicated Excuse for Everything
　in the Whole Wide World *Lesley Marshall*   77

It Wasn't Me *Steve Turner*   78

Tarzan Misses School *John C. Desmond*   79

Blame the Dog, Not Me! *Trevor Harvey*   80

No Hard Feelings *John Foster*   81

Animal Apologies *John Foster*   82

MISLEADING READING

Miss caught me scribbling on the desk
So I, while smiling sweetly,
Replied, 'I am not *scribbling*, Miss –
You'll find I'm writing NEATLY!'

GRAHAM DENTON

THE ASTRONAUT'S APOLOGY

Dear Moon, please ignore my exuberant jumps.
I should surely feel awed by your millions of lumps,
And those quirky rock ledges with dangerous edges
And craters that data just showed up as bumps.
I'm amazed, but I can't stop this bounding around,
Though my space-boots make prints in the dust of
   your ground,
For the joy I am jumping about is the view
Of dear Planet Earth with her oceans of blue.

PENNY DOLAN

tHe VaMPiRe'S APoloGY

'I didn't mean to cause offence,'
Said the vampire with a grin.
'But when I saw you'd cut your face,
I just had to lick your chin!'

JoHn FoSteR

THE LAST BOY to SCHOOL

The last boy to school
counts drifting sheep
between the dreaming clouds.

The last boy to school
follow snails' silver trails
down the slow winding path.

The last boy to school
feels each shade of green
that gleams in the glistening trees.

The last boy to school
sees no need
for the rulers,
the set squares, the text books:

his head is filled
with the whole of the world.

DAVE WARD

THIS IS WHY

The moon fell into my soup last night
with a plip and a plop and a wink.
It sang me a song of the evening star.
I didn't know what to think.

I should have been cleaning my room.
I promised my mother I would.
But the moon fell into my soup last night
and I didn't see how I could.

LINDA LEE WELCH

The Cloud's Lament

A cloud's gotta do what a cloud's gotta do!
You think we enjoy destroying the blue?
It's all right you pestering, 'Please don't rain!'
But clouds that don't burst are in awful pain.

It isn't as if we can choose where to go,
We're sent wherever the four winds blow.
The sun will always stand out from the crowd
But, rain or shine, a cloud is a cloud.

That's how it is and has always been
For us puddle-makers – it's not that we're mean,
We'd like you to play under skies of blue
But a cloud's do what a cloud's gotta do!

CELIA WARREN

OPEN HOUSE

Come round to my place
Whenever you like;
But maybe not Mondays,
I'm out on my bike.

And Tuesday's my scout night,
And Wednesday's the baths,
And Thursdays I have extra
Coaching in maths.

Not sure about Fridays;
Gran comes for a chat,
And Saturday's football;
I couldn't miss that.

Oh, maybe not Sundays –
We're out in the car.
But you're ALWAYS welcome;
You know that you are.

HAZEL TOWNSON

The Computer's Excuse for Crashing

You hit my keyboard far too hard,
The scanner's bruised,
My disk drive's scarred.

My monitor has greasy smears,
The printer's been
Reduced to tears.

And the mouse tells me your hands are rough,
He's very shy –
Enough's enough!

Those DVD horrors are starting to freak us,
And just when are you going
To dust the speakers?

My motherboard agrees you're mean,
So here's your reward:
The dreaded blue screen!

ANDY SEED

An Alien Ate My Homework

An Alien ate my homework.
I assure you, Miss, it's true.
I know you think I'm fibbing, Miss
But would I lie to you?

I'll tell you how it happened, Miss
I was alone last night.
I'd finished all my sums, Miss.
Yes, I *know* I got them right.

I was writing up my science
Which, quite frankly, Miss, was hard –
When a spaceship came and hovered
In the air above my yard!

A door slid slowly open, Miss,
And to my great surprise
I found myself regarded
By a pair of purple eyes.

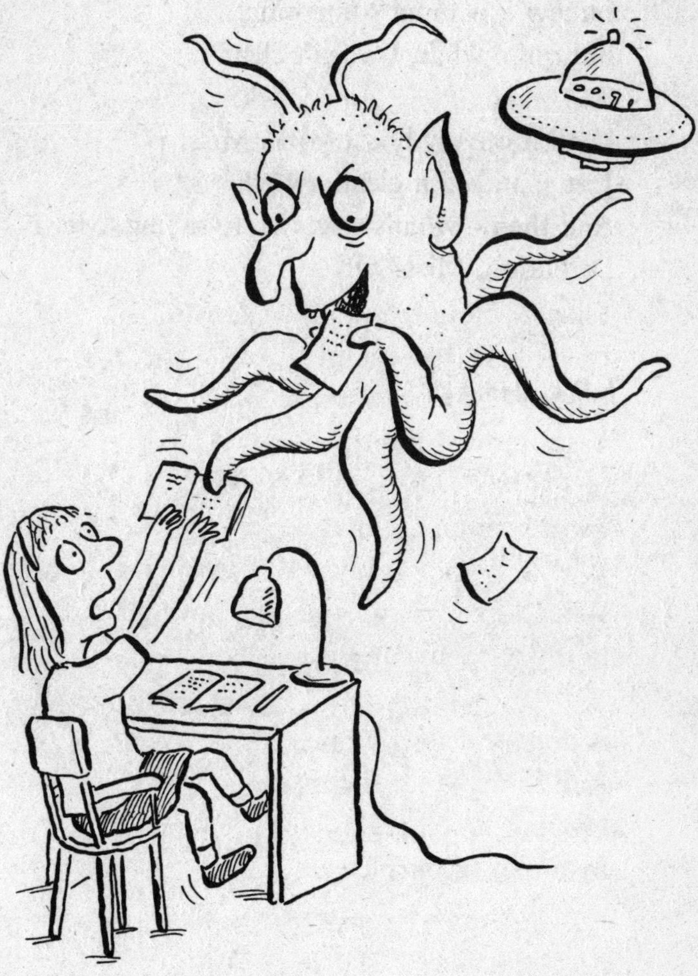

The thing was green, with tentacles.
My heart was filled with fear.
I knew it wanted something,
But quite what, I wasn't clear.

Until it ate my homework, Miss!
Just snatched it clean away!
And then – what's that you're saying, Miss?
Detention, Miss? OK.

KAYE UMANSKY

BARBARA IN THE SHED

That wasn't how it happened.
We told them we hadn't meant to do it.
I'm good at lies. I know how to mix them in with
    truth –
My dad's a brickie and I understand cement
'We never meant to lock her in.
The door stuck. I was playing with the bolt,
It cut my finger, look.' I lead them off the scent
With blood and rust, a feathered flap of skin.
Busy them with Savlon and Elastoplast.
'I'm sorry if we made her cry.' Another lie,
But sugared – her tears swamped by mine.
We'd loved it. Poking and stretching our faces into
    fangs.
And when we pushed her in the shed we danced
And hammered triumph on the walls.
That's the way it was.

JAN DEAN

NOTHING TO DO WITH ME

didn't see it

didn't read it

didn't hear it

didn't need it

didn't want it

didn't note it

didn't face it

didn't vote it

didn't love it

didn't hate it

didn't feel it

didn't rate it

didn't cop it

didn't knock it

didn't mean it

didn't stop it.

Jane Saddler

The Not-Me Kid

The Not-Me Kid
The Not-Me Kid
Said that he didn't
But of course he did
So he became
The Not-Me Kid.
That's his nickname:
The Not-Me Kid.

'Not me! Not me!'
We heard him claim.
Oh, but it was.
He knew no shame.
He'd not confess.
We knew his game.
Getting off lightly
Was his aim.

The Not-Me Kid
The Not-Me Kid
Said that he didn't
But of course he did
So he became
The Not-Me Kid.
That's his nickname:
The Not-Me Kid.

'I'm innocent!'
He'd still proclaim,
Though 'Wasn't me!'
Now sounded tame
Cos every time
We'd get the same
String of excuses
Each one lame.

The Not-Me Kid
The Not-Me Kid
Said that he didn't
But of course he did
So he became
The Not-Me Kid.
That's his nickname:
The Not-Me Kid.

Nick Toczek

ABSENCE

Dropped my sock
down the toilet.
I'm saving my jumper
so I won't spoil it.
My pants are worn out
and my shirt got chewed
by the dog
so I can't come to school
in the nude.

Jill Townsend

I'm Sorry That My Poem's Late

I'm sorry that
my poem's late;
I didn't quite
anticipate
that when I went
to write it down
I couldn't find
a single noun
Then (even worse
than I had feared)
I found my verbs
had disappeared.
A writing nightmare
coming true –
my adjectives
were missing too!

I scoured the house
for metaphors
and similes
behind the doors.
By now, I'm sure
that they were missing
like the rest.
And it was just
a waste of time
to look for rhythms,
or a rhyme.
I couldn't even
find a feeling,
though I searched
from floor to ceiling.

I didn't try
to understand,
but gripped my pencil
in my hand,
then set aside
my fear and rage
and pulled that pencil
down the page.
To my surprise,
the words flew out –
began to dance
and scream and shout.
Though I was mad,
I had to smile –
those silly words
were hiding in my pencil all the while.

TED SCHEU

THIS POEM SAYS SORRY

This poem says sorry
for its brevity of thought
Its one and only excuse
is that it's really quite short.

STEPHEN CLARKE

THAT'S NO EXCUSE!

Well, it *was*.

It might have been weak
And feeble and frail,
It might have been dopey
And doomed to fail;
Unconvincing perhaps,
Inadequate, lame,
It might have been flimsy,
It might have been tame.
I admit it was slender
And shifty and slight;
It could have been brainless
And not very bright.
OK – it was stupid
And not much use,
It was slim, it was dim –

But it *was* an excuse.

ERIC FINNEY

HERE LIES...

In life it's said, even as a youth,
He found it hard to tell the truth.
Meet him, he'd poke you in the ribs,
Laugh – and then start telling fibs.
On mobile phone or walkie-talkie
You'd hear him telling many a porky
And smooth as silk he could produce
Many a slippery excuse.
A whopper told, a tall tale spun:
That was his idea of fun.

In death, which now has come to claim him,
He's silent, so why should we blame him?
Of dead men we must not speak ill,
And yet it's true that he lies still.

ERIC FINNEY

The Conjuror's Ghost

'I'm sorry,' said the conjuror's ghost,
'I'm really in a fix.
I cannot fool the audience:
They see right through my tricks.'

John Foster

The Cow's Excuse

Hey diddle diddle
The cat and the fiddle
I was supposed to jump over the moon
But it *is* very high
And I can't really fly
Tho' I did think of using a balloon.

The dog thought it funny
But I hadn't the money
To buy a balloon – they're not cheap
So I stayed on the ground
(Much safer, I've found)
And visited Little Bo Peep.

Roger Stevens

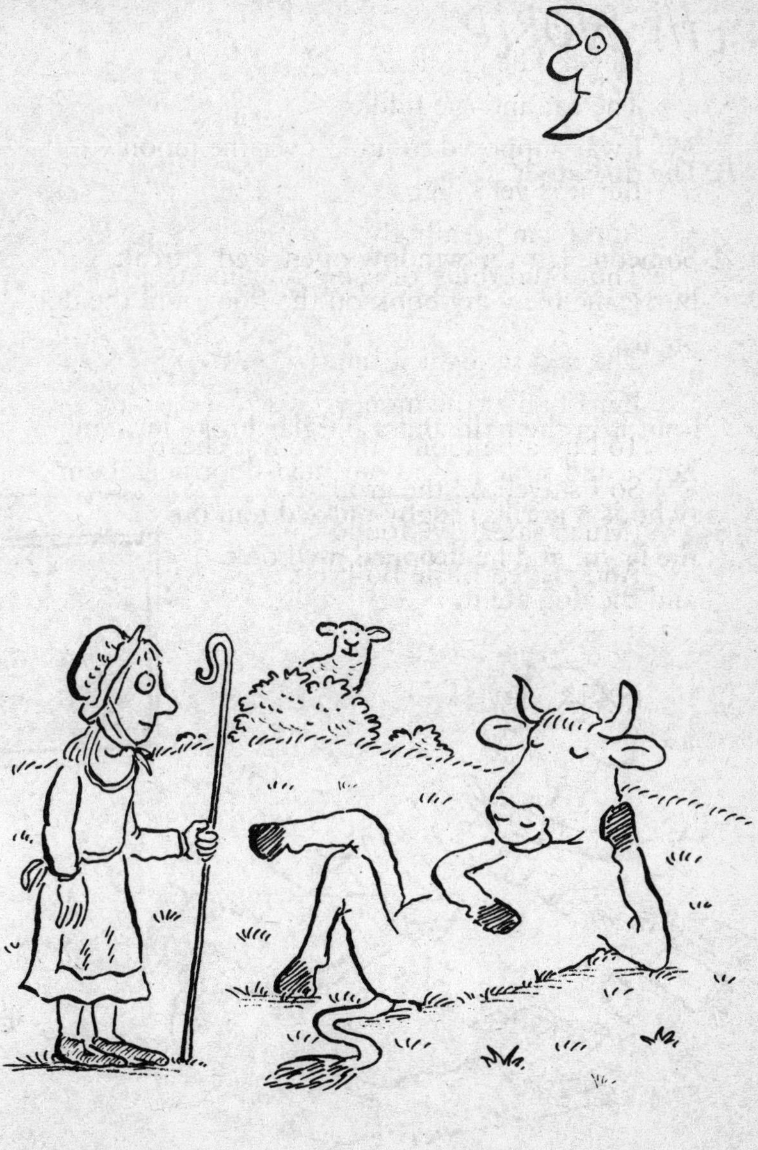

tHE WORSt EXCUSES in tHE WORLD

1. The dog ate it.

2. Someone left the window open, and a freak hurricane blew my book on the floor, and the dog ate it.

3. I put it in the hall, and a burglar broke into our house and stole it, and our next-door neighbour (who is a gorilla) rugby-tackled him on the lawn, and he dropped my book, and the dog ate it.

4. I'd just finished it when an extinct volcano at the end of the road suddenly erupted for the first time in ten million years and set fire to my book, and the firemen came and soaked it with their hoses, and as soon as it was dry the dog ate it.

5. I'd only left it for two minutes while I built a scale model of Buckingham Palace out of cheese triangles, when a whole herd of angry wildebeest stampeded through our back garden, battered down the kitchen door, and before they vanished into the shimmering sunset, they trampled my book under their mighty, thundering hooves, and the dog ate it.

6. Here is a big box of your favourite chocolates instead.

(Actually, THAT one works rather well.)

CLARE BEVAN

EXCUSE MY EXCUSE

Please excuse my excuse
And your excuse I'll excuse
But when words look the same
I often confuse
Excuse with excuse
And excuse with excuse.
I feel a bit silly,
And a bit of a goose
When I use the word excuse
Instead of excuse.
If these words looked different
We could all deduce
Which word was excuse
And which was excuse.
Until then we're tongue-tied
And it's really bad news
confusing excuse with excuse –
I mean excuse with excuse.

BRIAN PATTEN

WHO, ME?

You're mistaken.
I didn't start the war.

You're confusing me with someone else.
I'm a peacemaker.
Anyone will tell you that.

On the day war broke out
I was visiting sick people,
Raising money for one-eyed teddy bears,
And being nice to my mum.

Why are you looking at me like that?
Oh, all right then.
I admit it.

But it was only a tiny war.

Simon Pitt

A WAY WITH WORDS

The English books are handed out.
I open mine and scan the story
I wrote last week, 'The Robbers'.
Teacher has written in red biro,
'Well done. An excellent tale.
You have a way with words.'
And immediately
a memory stabs me in the back . . .

   . . . Paul and me
   at the newsagent's down the road,
   pocketing sweets from the Pick 'n' Choose corner.
   'Hey!' called the bald man behind the counter.
   'You two buying, or what?'
   'Just looking,' I answered
   and without a moment's hesitation
   went on to explain it was my mum's birthday soon
   and I was checking to see
   what sorts of sweets were in stock.
   The bald man nodded.
      A minute later
   we were out on the pavement.
   'You did it!' said Paul.
   'You got away . . . with words!'
   He grinned, and punched my shoulder.

    Those stolen sweets,
  just no way I could eat them.
  They burned a guilt hole in my pocket
  and I chucked them
    over a front garden hedge . . .

. . . 'Read us your story,' teacher orders,
and I stumble forward, stand before the class.
Paul grins, and gives me the double thumbs-up.
I look down at the 'The Robbers' in my English
    book,
see teacher's words written in red biro blood.
My eyes swim with water,
there's a lump in my throat
and I wish, I *wish* I could

get away from the words . . .

WES MAGEE

It's a Goal!

It may have been an own goal
But at least I scored,
Which is more than can be said
For the rest of the team.

JOHN HUNTER

REASONS WE CAN'T GET A DOG

We don't have a fence.
You wouldn't want him wandering off
on to the road, would you?
We have nowhere for him to sleep.
No, he couldn't sleep in your brother's bed.
All the snoring would keep him awake.
We have nothing to feed him.
Yes, you could feed him your vegetables,
but I don't think your mum would approve.
Besides, dogs scratch, bite, whimper,
howl at the moon.
Yes, I know your brother does too,
but we can't take him to the Refuge, can we?
And do you want the dog chasing poor Mrs Sims
and her cat down the road.
Yes, it would be funny. But not for Mrs Sims.
And don't say you have no one to play with.
What about me?
No, I won't fetch your ball, roll over or play dead!
No, we can't get a dog.

STEVEN HERRICK

Out of the Blue

I beg your pardon for dropping in
Unannounced and out of the blue
My manners may seem a little crude
But I'm a bomb – It's what I do.

Carefully crafted by expert hands
I'm top-of-the-range hardware
Unappreciated by those I visit
I'm a bringer of despair

I beg your pardon for dropping in
Unannounced and out of the blue
My manners may seem a little crude
But I'm a bomb – It's what I do.

I'll make my entrance through your roof
My once in a lifetime premiere
Socially outcast from all events
I'm a gatecrasher extraordinaire

I beg your pardon for dropping in
Unannounced and out of the blue
My manners may seem a little crude
But I'm a bomb – It's what I do.

I'm one of a kind, not built to last
No buy one get one free
Invite me in, we'll have a blast
What you get is what you see

I beg your pardon for dropping in
Unannounced and out of the blue
My manners may seem a little crude
But I'm a bomb – It's what I do.

DAMIAN HARVEY

Soldier, Soldier, Will You Marry Me?

Oh soldier, soldier, will you marry me,
With your musket, fife, and drum?
Oh no, pretty maid, I cannot marry you,
For I have no coat to put on.

Then away she went to the tailor's shop
As fast as legs could run,
And bought him one of the very very best,
And the soldier put it on.

Oh soldier, soldier, will you marry me,
With your musket, fife, and drum?
Oh no, pretty maid, I cannot marry you,
For I have no shoes to put on.

Then away she went to the cobbler's shop
As fast as legs could run,
And bought him a pair of the very very best,
And the soldier put them on.

Oh soldier, soldier, will you marry me,
With your musket, fife, and drum?
Oh no, pretty maid, I cannot marry you,
For I have no socks to put on.

Then away she went to the sock-maker's shop
As fast as legs could run,
And bought him a pair of the very very best,
And the soldier put them on.

Oh soldier, soldier, will you marry me,
With your musket, fife, and drum?
Oh no, pretty maid, I cannot marry you,
For I have no hat to put on.

Then away she went to the hatter's shop
As fast as legs could run,
And bought him one of the very very best,
And the soldier put it on.

Oh soldier, soldier, will you marry me,
With your musket, fife, and drum?
Oh no, pretty maid, I cannot marry you,
For I have a wife at home.

TRADITIONAL

GOLDFISH

I didn't feed you.
Nor did my brother.
Both of us thought
You were fed by the other.

RACHEL ROONEY

No Time

There's a poem in my biro,
there's a poem in my head,
but I can't sit down and write it –
I must go to school instead.
Then after school it's football
and I can't let down the team.
If I don't get my homework done
my mum will start to scream.
There's a poem in my biro,
there's a poem in my head,
but my favourite show's on telly
and it's nearly time for bed.
I must go on the computer,
and I said I'd ring my gran
to thank her for my present
and to tell her how I am.
There's a poem in my biro,
there's a poem in my head.
If I can't find time to write it
it must always stay unread.

Alison Chisholm

WHO WAS SUPPOSED to FEED tHE HAMStER?

'Well, you see, Miss,
It was like this, Miss.
    I'm not talking to Chloe
    And Chloe's not talking to Jill
    and Jill's not talking to Zoe
    And Zoe's not talking to Will
    And Will's not talking to Harry
    And Harry's not talking to Tim
    And Tim's not talking to Larry
    And Larry's not talking to Jim.
    And Jim's not talking to Amy
    And Amy's not talking to Rick
    And Rick's not talking to Maimie
    And Maimie's not talking to Flick
    And Flick's not talking to Molly
    And Molly's not talking to Dee
    And Dee's not talking to Holly
    And Holly's not talking to ME

SO – nobody
Told anybody
That somebody
Had to feed
The hamster
Today.

Sorry!'

JENNIFER CURRY

OH, AM I STILL HERE?

Oh, am I still here?
I thought that I was up.
I thought I was
    doing the dishes
    ironing the budgie
    and wallpapering the cat.
What me – *skiving*?
Reading when I should be up and at?
Now would I do a thing like that?

Oh, am I still here?
I thought that I was hard at work
    planting the baby
    hoovering a raspberry jelly
    taking next-door's curtains for a walk . . .
I know that there are THINGS TO DO.
And I must deal with SERIOUS STUFF
But somehow, nothing's serious enough
To drag me out of this great story that I'm in.

So you can stand there and complain
As loud and crazy as you like.
Go on – if it makes you feel good – rant and shout.
BUT I'M INSIDE THIS BOOK AND I'M NOT
   COMING OUT!

Jan Dean

THIS POEM APOLOGIZES

This poem apologizes
It does not offer credit
it is not a lotto ticket
it has not got your name on it
and it will not make you rich.

This poem apologizes.
It is not an exam paper, a passport
a quiz, a query, a questionnaire –
it will not get you anywhere.

This poem apologizes
for delays caused by faults on the line
and for not keeping to time,

this poem is not an excuse note, a love letter
a shopping list, a weather forecast
a prescription to make you better
an airline ticket, first class,
a visa or an exam reviser –

no, it is none of these
but a poem
making lines and rhymes
and hoping you'll hear them.

This poem apologizes
for all the things
it might have been
and might have done.
This poem begs your pardon.

HELEN DUNMORE

An Easy Mistake

Terence the tiger
ate poor little Fred,
burped, licked his whiskers
and soulfully said:

'When he held out a Mars bar
I thought it was starters,
with Fred for main course
... *now, what's for afters?*'

Patricia Leighton

BROKEN PROMISE

My mum has a fine china shepherdess
Which she dusts with feathers of hate
It came with an excuse and apologies
When Dad came home several days late.

LUCINDA JACOB

The Spider's Excuse

I'm a little spider.
Be not afraid, for I am good.
I wouldn't hurt a fly.
No. That's not true. I would.

Steve Turner

THE ELASTIC'S APOLOGY

I realize it was embarrassing
That I snapped in the middle of town.
But I've been frayed for ages.
I'm sorry I let you down.

JOHN FOSTER

WHY ARE YOU LATE FOR SCHOOL?

I didn't get up
because I was too tired
and I was too tired
because I went to bed late
and I went to bed late
because I had homework
and I had homework
because the teacher made me
and the teacher made me
because I didn't understand
and I didn't understand
because I wasn't listening
and I wasn't listening
because I was staring out of the window
and I was staring out of the window
because I saw a cloud.
I am late, sir,
because I saw a cloud.

Steve Turner

EXCUSES, EXCUSES

He plots in the early dawn
I can't go to school, Mum
My head aches
I feel sick
Don't make me go.

He rehearses as the day breaks
I can't go to school, Mum
I've lost my PE kit
I haven't done my homework
Don't make me go.

He pleads over breakfast
I can't go to school, Mum
My stomach hurts
You don't understand
Don't make me go.

As she turns away annoyed,
he whispers . . .
They'll be waiting for me.

CATHARINE BODDY

i Don't Be-Leaf You

Oi you! Yes, you! The one wearing green,
Skulking there by that gate, trying not to be seen.
Don't you know you're unwelcome, you hulking great lout!
So shove off right now, and quit hanging about.
And as for that footwear, those scruffy brown boots,
Don't try to confuse me by calling them roots!
And pick up that litter you've scattered around,
All those tatty green wrappers you've chucked on the ground.
Your hair's in a state, lad, I can't see your face,
I suppose it's the fashion to look a disgrace.
You what? Didn't catch that. A trick of the light?
And that's your excuse: *You're a tree!* Huh! Yeah, right!

POLLY PETERS

BLACK-EYED SUSAN

What do you want,
A porky pie?
A seagull doop
Fell from the sky.
The table and I
Had an argument.
I practised snogging
Patricia Pavement.
I painted these bruises
just for the crack.
It's genetic, my eyes
Have always been black.

What do you want?
The truth of this crime?
My dad will deny it
Every time.

ANDREW FUSEK PETERS

tHE SLiPPERY tRutH
(tHE BANANA'S EXCUSE)

Blame the dad
Who bought a bunch.
Blame the girl
Who peeled her lunch.

Blame the bin
That nearly caught it,
Blame the breeze
That flung and fought it.

Blame the boy
Who didn't see
Where it sat
Innocently.

Blame the air
On which he flew
All the way to
Timbuktu.

But never blame
the trouble he's in
on humble old
banana skin.

ANDREW FUSEK PETERS

A Note From Mum

I'm sorry there's nothing
for breakfast.
I'm sorry there's nothing to eat.
There isn't much more
for dinner.
I've simply been rushed
off my feet.

I'm sorry your clothes
are all dirty
The washing machine's
gone wrong.
I'm just popping out for
some shopping.
I promise I won't
be long.

I'm sorry I wasn't
back sooner.
I met Mrs Jones
in the street.
I helped her home with
her shopping.
She was overcome by
the heat.

I'm sorry, I'm sorry,
I'm sorry.
Forgive me for all
I don't do.
Can a working mum,
so busy,
be excused? When she
loves you?

PS

I'm cooking a slap-up
supper.
A little bit late
I agree.
Stir-fry chicken and oodles
of noodles.
Things *will* get better,
you'll see!

Ann Bonner

A Sorry Story
(Following A School Trip to the Jolly Roger)

'Sorry!' boomed the Pirate,
'Sorry!' squawked his bird,
'We've gone and taught the infants
A rather naughty word.

'We've gone and forced your teachers
To walk the wooden plank,
We've gone and danced a hornpipe
While all their handbags sank.

'We've gone and sent your helpers
A-swinging from the sails,
We've gone and fed your worksheets
To hungry sharks and whales.

'We've gone and wrecked your outing
(A shocking thing to do.)'
'Forget it,' yelled the children.
'We want to join the crew!'

Clare Bevan

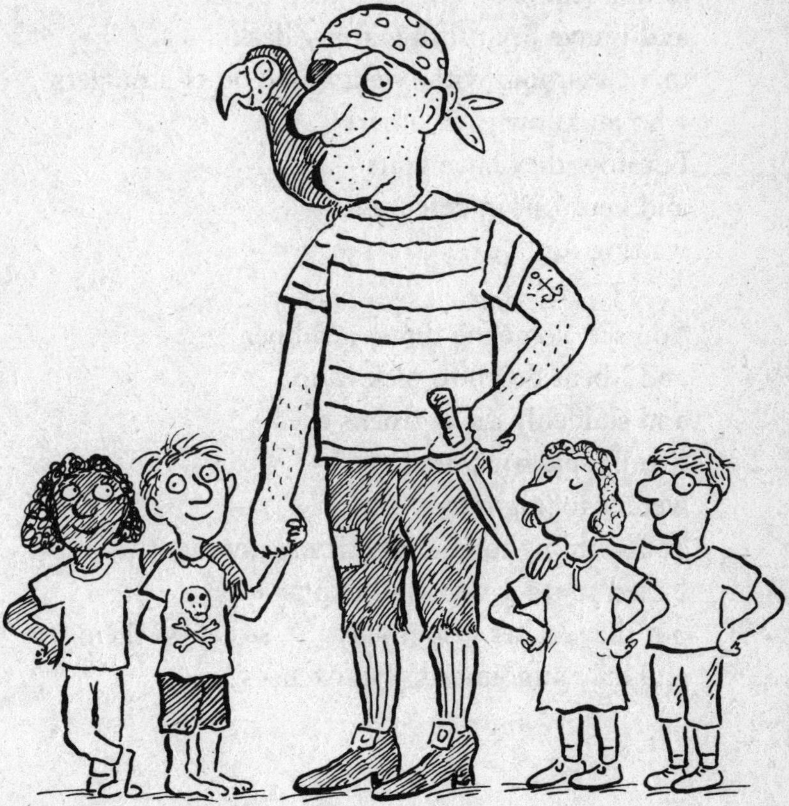

Waiting for the Eyes to Return

I'm the Lone Ranger,
a complete stranger
in this school
and I have been sitting at my desk
in a classroom with twenty-nine other strangers
who all know each other!
But now they have gone
and here I sit in detention
waiting for . . .

You see, someone threw a rubber
and I bent down to pick it up
and suddenly the teacher's eyes
– unhappy, frustrated eyes –
were stabbing mine
and with my tongue not fitting my mouth
I tried to offer words of explanation
but the teacher just cruelly . . . stood on them
and icily announced, 'No excuses!'

And now I am in detention
where the silence is very uncomfortable
and the sunshine has rushed out of the room
and the desks have quietly surrounded me.
I am waiting, waiting for the eyes to return!

Ian Souter

tHE WOLF'S EXCUSE

Would it be too crass
To apologize
To the girl, and her family, and you?
Yet – I was hungry,
And I'm a wolf,
It's what we do.

Gran was like leather,
Tough as old boots,
She had to be chewed with great care.
Then came the knocking
On the cottage door,
'Gran, are you there?'

You could call it greed.
I had eaten once,
And I shouldn't have taken the bait.
But here she was,
Fresh, tender young meat
On a red plate.

I believe it was fate
That brought her there,
And I ate her without much ado.
For I *was* hungry,
And I *am* a wolf.
It's what we do.

YVONNE COPPARD

A Diner Apologizes

I'm terribly sorry I ate you
but you had a delectable smell.
It must be so awfully upsetting
and me on a diet as well.

I promised myself I'd stop snacking
and exercise some self-control
but my meals, of late, have been so meagre,
there you were, so tender, so whole.

It's really hard work cutting out things,
those goodies which make the mouth drool.
Look, I'm doing my best to say sorry,
it's not true that I'm vicious and cruel.

So believe me, you were delicious,
organic and additive free,
with a taste which I really did relish,
and presented so exquisitely.

I'm terribly sorry I ate you
but deep down the ocean is dark,
and you shouldn't have come in the water.
So what do you expect from a shark?

STEWART HENDERSON

A WASHING MACHINE APOLOGIZES

I'm sorry if I:

> Creased your shirts
> Wrecked your skirts,
> Tore your tights,
> Spoiled your whites,
> Turned them pink,
> Made them shrink,
> And flooded the lobby.

I'm sorry that I:

    Ate your socks,
    Chewed your frocks,
    Mangled clothes,
    Clogged my hose,
    Learned to squeak,
    Sprang a leak,
    But hey! It's my hobby.

Clare Bevan

First Things First

'Can't do it now, my precious,'
He told his darling missus
When she asked her loving hubby
To wash the dirty dishes.

'Too busy, pet,' he told her,
'Important work to do –
I'm counting grass blades on the lawn
In case we've got too few . . .'

Clive Webster

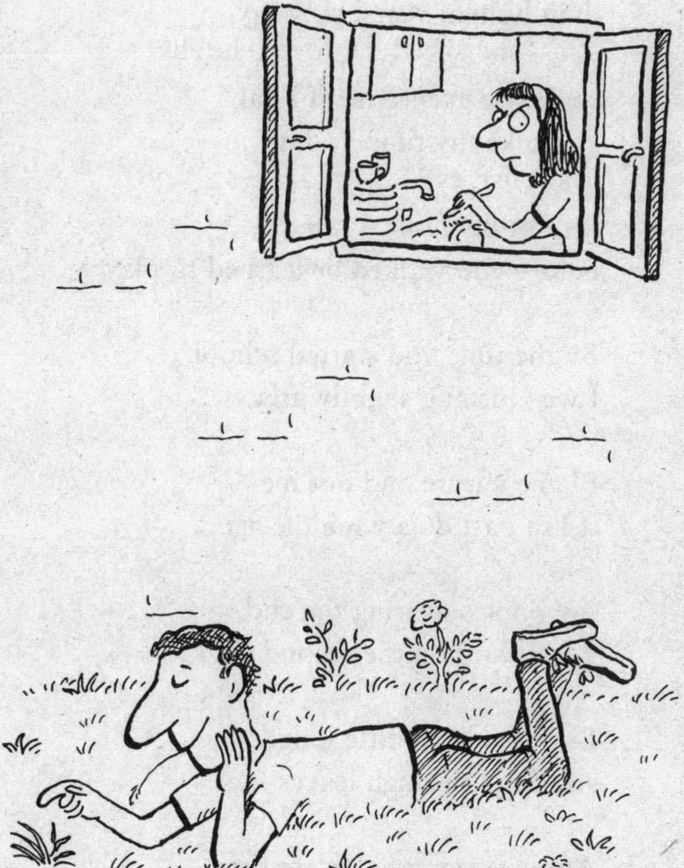

WALKIES

Dog years tick tock tick quicker
than human years, they say,

so please excuse me if I pant
and take my time, today:

it's not my fault. I *ran*
before you walked or learned to play.

By the time you started school,
I was turning slightly grey.

Blame nature and not me
if I'm past doggy middle age;

my book's nearing the end,
you're still on the second page.

Let me sniff a little longer,
shuffling through leaves –

Autumn is my favourite time . . .
Soon spring's blooms you'll breathe:

think of me, as you walk here, then,
our marvellous memories;

all that fun together, running,
chasing round those trees!

Yes, there's a reason why I'll pant
and take my time, today:

dog years tick tock tick quicker
than human years, they say.

Mike Johnson

too risky

He'd made excuses before, of course,
But this one took the biscuit –
'My parakeet's got housemaid's knee,
I don't think I can risk it.'

CLIVE WEBSTER

Writer's Excuse

My head doth ache,
My hand doth shake,
   I have a naughty pen;
My ink is bad,
My pen is worse,
   How can I write well then?

Traditional

One, Two, Three, Four, Five

One, two, three, four, five,
Once I caught a fish alive,
Why did you let it go?
Because it bit my finger so.

Six, seven, eight, nine, ten,
Shall we go to fish again?
Not today, some other time,
For I have broke my fishing line.

Traditional

THE MOST COMPLICATED EXCUSE FOR EVERYTHING IN THE WHOLE WIDE WORLD

I lent Ben my torch
so that he could finish the book that
Phoebe is going to lend me next
but Ben says he swapped it
for a go on Kelly's Game Boy.

But Kelly left the torch on all night
which made the batteries run out
so she says she swapped Harry a pack of cards
for some batteries that her dad
has put in his recharger overnight.

So whilst I'm waiting for the batteries to recharge
for Kelly to use the torch
and Ben to play the Game Boy
and Phoebe to lend me the book

I'm sitting twiddling my thumbs on my own
in a bad mood in the dark.

LESLEY MARSHALL

It Wasn't Me

It wasn't me, my cup just fell,
The plate jumped on the floor,
The window cracked all by itself
And then it slammed the door.

I didn't punch, my hand just slipped
And curled into a fist.
He happened to come walking by,
I happened not to miss.

It wasn't me who talked in class,
I didn't steal that pen,
If someone says they saw me cheat
They've got it wrong again.

It wasn't me, it's not my fault!
Why do I get the blame?
The naughty child who does these things
Has pinched my face and name.

Steve Turner

TARZAN MISSES SCHOOL

Your excuses for absence
over the past year just will not do.

Theft in the kangaroo enclosure –
all pouches had to be searched.

Polar bear, having lost his compass,
to be brought back from the South Pole.

Badly bitten feeding the pigeons;
even if it was to the lions.

Helping an uptight anaconda unwind.
Wiping crocodiles' tears. Walking the goldfish.

And this last one is no excuse at all –
having a laugh with the hyenas.

JOHN C. DESMOND

BLAME tHE DOG, NOt ME!

It was FIDO who broke the remote control
And spilt yogurt all over the floor!
It was FIDO who managed to kick the ball
And shatter a window next door!
It was FIDO who tore your library book
(He's becoming a TERRIBLE ripper)!
It wasn't ME! You've made a mistake –

I was busy, chewing your slipper . . .

TREVOR HARVEY

NO HARD FEELINGS

'I'm sorry,' said the apple
As it bounced off Newton's head.
'I didn't see you standing there.
You really should have said.'

'Don't apologize,' said Newton
'Although my head is sore,
You have shown me that gravity
Is just a natural law.'

JOHN FOSTER

ANIMAL APOLOGIES

'Sorry,' said the kangaroo.
'I shouldn't have jumped to conclusions.'

'Sorry,' said the camel.
'I can't help it. I've always got the hump.'

'Sorry,' said the dog.
'I've been barking up the wrong tree.'

'Sorry,' said the electric eel.
'I've got my wires crossed.'

'Sorry,' said the donkey.
'I'm always making an ass of myself.'

'Sorry,' said the giraffe.
'I shouldn't have stuck my neck out.'

'Sorry,' said the crocodile.
'I shouldn't have snapped.'

JOHN FOSTER

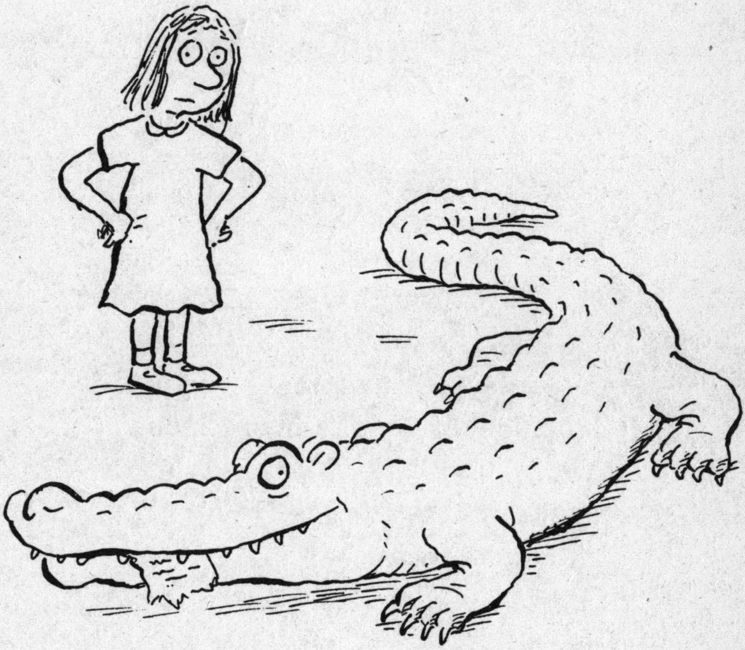

Kick It!
Football poems by Nick Toczek

Kick It! is a fantastic collection of energetic football poems from master rhymer Nick Toczek exploring every area of our favourite game. Meet 'The Football Family Man' and 'The Kick It Kid', find out about 'The World's First Football' and 'Why Groundsmen Never Relax', but most of all believe him when he tells you that 'A Football is the Ball for Me'!

from **A Football is the Ball for Me**

Though netball's cool and baseball's slick,

There's only one ball game they just can't lick.

I want a ball, a ball, a ball you can kick.

There's just one game with which I click.

Football, through thin and thick.

Football wins my voting tick.

Football, or my name's not Nick.

So I want a ball,
  A real ball,
    A proper ball
      A ball you can kick.

Spectacular Schools

poems chosen by
Paul Cookson and David Harmer

Sneak a peek into the craziest classrooms ever! Find out what snowmen learn and sing the dragon school song. Discover how to become a pirate, and which vampire school to choose. You'll never look at your own school in the same way again!

from
Circus School Reception Class

My little brother Adam
has started circus school.

He's learning to juggle two teddy bears
and to throw rubber knives at a wooden man.

For homework he balanced
Mum and Grandma on his head.

Next year he's in Year One
doing lion taming.

David Harmer

A selected list of titles available from Macmillan Children's Books

The prices shown below are correct at the time of going to press. However, Macmillan Publishers reserve the right to show new retail prices on covers which may differ from those previously advertised.

A Nest Full of Stars	0 330 39752 4	£4.99
I Did Not Eat the Goldfish	0 330 39718 4	£3.99
The Very Best of Paul Cookson	0 330 48014 6	£3.99
The Very Best of Wes Magee	0 330 48192 4	£3.99
Don't Get Your Knickers in a Twist	0 330 39769 9	£3.99
Ye New Spell Book	0 330 39708 7	£3.99
The Colour of My Dreams	0 330 48020 0	£4.99
Taking My Human for a Walk	0 330 39871 7	£3.99
The Rhyme Riot	0 330 39900 4	£3.50
The Horrible Headmonster	0 330 48489 3	£3.50
You're Not Going Out Like That!	0 330 39846 6	£3.99
My Stepdad's an Alien	0 330 41552 2	£3.99
The Teacher's Revenge	0 330 39901 2	£3.99
Wallpapering the Cat	0 330 39903 9	£4.99
One River, Many Creeks	0 330 39768 0	£4.99

All Macmillan titles can be ordered from our website,
www.panmacmillan.com,
or from your local bookshop and are also available by post from:

Bookpost, PO Box 29, Douglas, Isle of Man IM99 1BQ

Credit cards accepted. For details:
Telephone: 01624 836000
Fax: 01624 670923
E-mail: bookshop@enterprise.net
www.bookpost.co.uk

Free postage and packing in the United Kingdom